IMAGES OF ENGLAND

HALIFAX
REVISITED

IMAGES OF ENGLAND

HALIFAX
REVISITED

VERA CHAPMAN

The
History
Press

Frontispiece: Halifax Town Hall from Princess Street, *c.* 1905.

First published in 2003
Reprinted 2011

The History Press
The Mill, Brimscombe Port,
Stroud, Gloucestershire, GL5 2QG
www.thehistorypress.co.uk

© Vera Chapman, 2003, 2011

British Library Cataloguing in Publication Data.
A catalogue record for this book is available from the British Library.

ISBN 978 0 7524 3047 8

Typesetting and origination by The History Press
Printed in Great Britain

Contents

Timber-framed house in Shibden Hall Park. (Courtesy of Frank Atkinson)

Introduction

Halifax, the 'hilly-milly' town, is where I was born. I remember it best from the years between the First and Second World Wars. It seemed an exciting place as I used to shuttle between Boothtown and Pellon to visit my relatives, walking down the cat-steps path into the Hebble Valley bottom, past the mill ponds, under the Woodside Viaduct, into the Wheatley Valley, up a steep diagonal path to Queen's Road and Pellon – or down Haley Hill or Pellon Lane to visit the town centre.

I knew it as a town and district of precipitous slopes and deep valleys, of mist-shrouded, snow-covered moors and windswept, rain-soaked hills. Trade had been along packhorse tracks across the heights. Wool had been handspun and woven in hillside homes, where now the signs of seventeenth-century prosperity survive in the handsome 'Halifax Houses', the ruins thereof or in museums.

In the eighteenth century, turnpike roads came to the valleys, with better surfaces and gentler gradients, signposting and distance-marking. Came, too, navigations and canals, and water wheels and steam for powering spinning and weaving machines. All these promoted a revolution, not only in industry but also domesticity as a movement downward began to harness the water in these ice-scoured valleys. Shallow coal seams were mined to convert water to steam and a forest of tall chimneys sprouted along the riversides as shown dramatically in this album.

The nineteenth century railways reinforced the new pattern as they pierced the hills via lengthy tunnels and crossed the valleys by spectacular embankments and viaducts. Wharves and stations with new settlements spawned in the valley bottoms below the old villages, the mills spreading along the watersides like strings of beads, but of jet rather than pearls. Yet there were wooded patches in between, and countryside and moorland never far away.

The old forests had long-since gone, and the sturdy timber-framed houses that might have lasted for centuries were unappreciated. Only a few were preserved as museum pieces or *in situ*. But the tough gritstones of the hills were excellent for building the villas and terraces of the burgeoning town, and the fireclay seams could provide pipes for water and sanitation. Beacon Hill limited town expansion on that side, so the suburbs grew westward and into the freshening breezes.

There seem to have been two periods of especial prosperity based on woollens and worsteds: the seventeenth and the nineteenth centuries. From the mid-nineteenth the wealthy families and Halifax Corporation set about to improve conditions in the town itself. So the ancient green and markets and the narrow central streets were opened out with new streets and buildings and a Town Hall and Borough Market. The gardens of prominent citizens became public parks. Industry diversified, especially into confectionery, financial services, entertainment and tourism. The massive mills of the Hebble Valley were refurbished for modern uses. Sub-standard property was demolished and soot-stained buildings cleaned. Even the cooling towers have come and gone! The once-industrial countryside is now crisscrossed with walkers' footpaths and nature trails. Halifax has changed – but still excites me!

Vera Chapman
July, 2003

one

Industrial
Halifax

Halifax from Beacon Hill, *c.* 1916. On the left, Horton Street leads from Wards End to Halifax joint station with platform canopies on the left and sidings on the right. Square old and new chapels and the Piece Hall are centre and distant right is the Town Hall steeple. To the right is the parish church. One railway line curves off to Beacon Hill tunnel, the other to North Bridge and the Hebble Valley. In the foreground are mills at Bailey Hall and Clark Bridge.

Pellon from Woodside, 1942. In the terrace just beyond the mill ponds and railway viaduct, the the lower storeys opened to the road and tramway to Ovendon, the upper storeys to Old Lee Bank behind. Distant Pellon stands high above the Wheatley valley. (Field sketch by Vera Chapman, neé Taylor)

Sketch of Halifax town, from a lane above Claremount Road, 1942. All Souls' church spire, Haley Hill, is at the centre. As many as fifty mill chimneys rose in the valley below the town. (Sketch by Vera Chapman)

Halifax from Beacon Hill. Charlestown Road curves from the foot of Beacon Hill, parallel with the railway viaduct from Halifax station to North Bridge station, continuing as Haley Hill. All Souls church is clearly visible. Haley Hill and Dean Clough Mills are on the left.

Dean Clough Mills. John Crossley (1772–1837) began carpet making here in 1803. His three sons John, Joseph and Francis eventually expanded it to seven large mills employing around 5,000 workers – reputedly the world's largest carpet factory.

J. and J. Baldwin, later Patons and Baldwins. Clark Bridge Mills at Bank Bottom were founded in 1785 for the production of woollen and worsted yarns. Expanded to accommodate a workforce of around 3,000, the cramped conditions led to a move in 1947, with its partner firms in Scotland and Leicestershire, to a greenfield site at Darlington, thus becoming the world's largest knitting yarn factory. (This series of photographs is courtesy of Coats Crafts UK, Darlington)

Another of the Baldwins' later Clark Bridge Mills buildings. Dr Joe Gaunt, dyes chemist, and works engineers lived in tied houses at the base of the works' chimney. Betty Gaunt remembers sooty grit falling on to her washing and the steep climb with prams to go shopping in town beyond the viaduct!

The cover of a Baldwins' brochure.

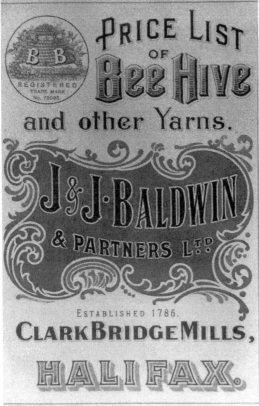

Above: Detail from Baldwins' brochure. Clergy (clerks or clarks) from Wakefield Cathedral crossed the Hebble at Clark Bridge to reach the parish church and Market via Woolshops.

Left: A Beehive price list. The well-known trade mark of the two Baldwins no doubt implied a busy firm. John Baldwin became the first mayor of Halifax in 1848. He left his Spring Hall estate to the town.

Opposite above: J. and J. Baldwin and Partners. Blending wools at Halifax. Many different animal and man-made fibres were used.

Opposite below: Packing parcels of yarn at Halifax.

BROOKES'
LTD.

SETTS,
MACADAM,
KERB,
BUILDING
STONE,
DOCK WORK,
&c., &c.

Chief Office : HALIFAX.

AND AT

LONDON,
MANCHESTER,
ABERDEEN, CONWAY,
GUERNSEY,
ALDERNEY, NORWAY,
SWEDEN.

3rd INTERNATIONAL ROAD CONGRESS EXHIBITION, LONDON, JUNE, 1913.

Dealers in stone. Brookes' Ltd had their chief office in Halifax, appropriately as the quarrying of sandstone, gritstone and flagstone (and fireclay) was an important but scattered industry in the area. Builders took advantage of the wealthy industrialists and merchants who desired fine houses and premises in an expanding town.

The former Bowling Dyke Mills and dye works from Cross Hills Road, 2003. The Hebble Valley bottom upstream of North Bridge became choked with mills. Colonel Akroyd had one here and another across Haley Hill Road on his Akroydon estate. Upstream were Crossleys Dean Clough Mills below Woodside. Most are now revamped for business, the arts, health and a hotel.

John Mackintosh and Sons. John (1868-1920) and his new wife Violet opened a confectionery shop in King Cross Street in 1890. Their butterscotch and caramel was so successful that they developed factories and warehouses to cater for the wholesale market. After a Queens Road factory fire in 1911 they moved to a site behind Halifax station, producing wrapped and tinned toffee. Caley's chocolate firm was acquired, and chocolate and toffees like Quality Street and Rolo were produced. A merger with Rowntree took place in 1969, and the company was then bought by Nestlé in 1988. Around 2,500 people were employed in Halifax's renovated factory.

Riley's Hanson Lane Toffee Mills. This Edwardian business card features nonslip stone flag flooring at Riley's. Elland flags were crushed to make artificial stone, which can sometimes be seen in town pavements with metal labels reading 'NONSLIP HALIFAX' punched into them. On outings with my grandma and aunts, a Riley's Toffee Roll would ensure that I was a good girl!

The Halifax Permanent Benefit Building Society. This company began trading in the Oak Room at the Old Cock inn in Southgate in 1852, and moved to buildings near the Town Hall in around 1871. In 1927 it merged with the Halifax Equitable Building Society and moved to York Buildings on Commercial Street. Between 1968 and 1974 it moved to its acutely modern new national headquarters building in Trinity Road. In 1995 it merged with Leeds Permanent Building Society and became a Public Limited Company in 1997. It also has a computerised database at Copley.

Halifax Building Society's local main branch is in York Buildings, Commercial Street. This was built in 1905 for Alexander Scott Ltd, silk mercers, drapers, hosiers, dressmakers and milliners. The Society re-fronted it and added the coupled black granite pillars. At least five generations of my family have saved or loaned with the Halifax!

'Courierites' at Windermere. At centre is the lad John Taylor. His family had moved to Halifax from Oldham during the cotton depression of the 1890s. He attended Pellon Lane school from the age of nine. At thirteen he got work in the *Halifax Courier* office, but was offered only a boy's job with no further prospects. Later, however, he was put 'upstairs' as an apprentice. In 1901, news came at around 6 p.m. of Queen Victoria's death. All the paper boys had long-since taken out the last edition, so the office boys and apprentices were sent out with 'specials' which sold like hot cakes. John sold twenty dozen!

John Taylor at a linotype machine. The *Halifax Courier* was published weekly on Saturdays and the *Halifax Evening News* daily. The hot metal process punched letters and words onto metal bars which were assembled into lines and pages in frames. Having served his apprenticeship, a vacancy came up and John served the company for twenty-five years. He enjoyed cycling and watching rugby at Thrum Hall and the Shay grounds as hobbies.

Above: A presentation clock. The inscription reads: 'Presented to Mr John Taylor by his Fellow Employees in the *Halifax Courier* and *Guardian* on severing his connection with the firm after twenty-five years service, July 6 1923'. He went to work with Kemsley Newspapers at Withy Grove, Manchester as a linotype operator until retirement.

Left: Joe Lister was a fellow linotype operator at the *Courier*, and when he left for America on Boxing Day (probably around 1913) John 'took his machine'. They corresponded until Joe reached the age of eighty-two.

two

Bygone
Scenes

Old Market in 1835. In the foreground are bolts of cloth. The three soldiers are in the uniform of the Halifax Volunteers. (This and the following five images are taken from Stoddart's 'Old Halifax' series of prints by John Horner, reproduced as Edwardian postcards)

Old Market and Corn Market.

Above left: Old Market and part of Crown Street.

Above right: Crown Street, south side.

Below: Silver Street, 1868. Seen from Hall End, it shows the Commercial Bank, the White Lion and the Globe inn.

Opposite above: Hall End showing portions of Silver Street, Copper Street and Swine Market.

Opposite below: The Lower Market, from a pencil drawing by C. Crossley.

Right: Cheapside, from a pencil drawing by C. Crossley.

Below: The Royal Oak, from a pencil drawing by C. Crossley.

The Old Talbot, from an etching by C. Crossley.

Site of the old gibbet on Halifax Green (Cow Green). Later a platform and steps were built at Gibbet Hill. It was then sited in the back garden of a house on a corner of Bedford Street North. Originally an iron axe was suspended between two tall posts. Fifty cloth-stealers were executed between 1550 and 1650.

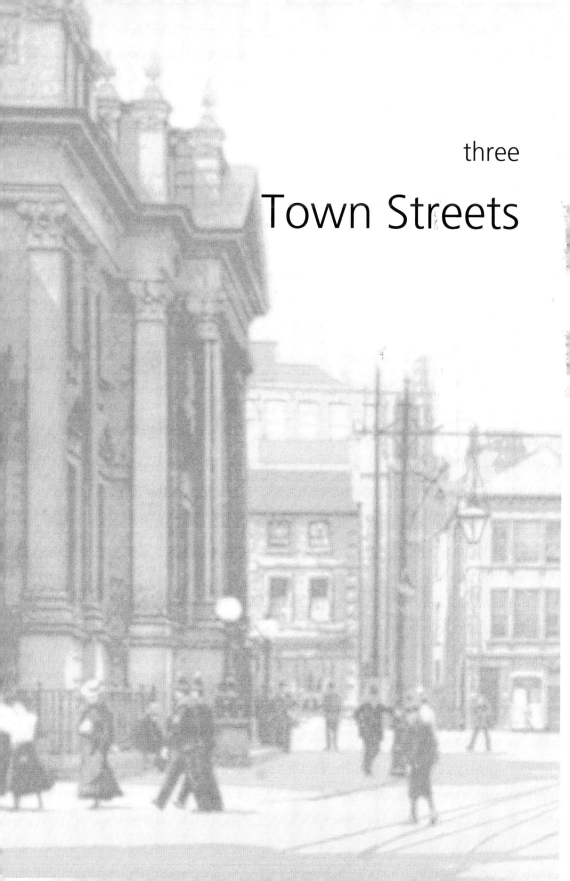

three

Town Streets

Commercial Street from the south end. This broad business street was developed from 1880, and the growth continued over the next two decades. On the right, the Halifax Permanent Benefit Building Society occupies York House, built in 1904-1905, which it re-fronted.

Commercial Street from Ward's End. The Victoria Hall on the left was built in 1900. The hoarding on the right (just seen) marks the site of York House, which at this time was yet to be built.

Commercial Street, looking north, showing fine shops and office blocks. Rule and Dixon's grocery shop on the right had the Refuge Assurance offices above. York House has yet to be built. The buildings are not yet smoke-blackened! Dean Clough Mills can be seen in the hazy distance. The electric tram network came in 1898-1905.

Commercial Street. The view is looking north. The area was redeveloped at about the same time as Leeds' Briggate and Vicar Lane, with turrets, towers and steep roofs a feature. Rule and Dixon's corner grocery shop is on the right.

Commercial Street, east side. Turrets can be seen here, too. The Halifax and Huddersfield Union Banking Company, at an angle between Rawson Street and George Street, has a fine frontage with green marble pillars. Built in 1898 for an amalgam of earlier banking companies, it continued with several mergers.

Commercial Street from George Street. The post office opposite was a popular subject for photographers.

Commercial Street. The post office was built in 1887 to the design of Henry Tanner of HM Board of Works, who also designed Leeds post office in City Square. Nicholl and Brown's shop name draws attention because of its venturesome lettering.

Commercial Street looking north from the post office, *c.* 1903. At the end is the site of the old Cloth Hall, now a busy junction with Silver Street, Crown Street and Waterhouse Street.

Left: Sunday evening in Commercial Street meant parading in best clothes and meeting friends. My cousins called it mashing!

Below: Wards End. The picture house on the left opened in 1913 showing silent films. Talkies came in the 1920s. It was renamed the Gaumont, then the Astra, closing in 1982, soon to become the Coliseum with dancing and bars. The Victoria Hall opened in 1901 with a concert in memory of the late Queen. Miss Porter donated the grand organ. From the 1960s it was the Civic Theatre, with 1,600 seats. The Regal cinema came to the empty site (far right).

Above: Wards End. The Palace Music Hall on the right was designed by Ernest Runtz, built 1900–1903, demolished in 1959 and replaced by an office and shops development. On Saturdays my uncle Tom Park used to watch football in the afternoon, go to a show at the Palace in the evening and pick up a cheap rabbit near closing time in the Borough Market on the way home!

Right: This postcard advertised Mr Horace Hodges as *Grumpy*, by Horace Hodges and T. Wigney Percyval by arrangement with Mr Cyril Maude, which showed for six nights at the Theatre Royal. This elegant theatre opposite the Palace was designed by Horsfall, opened in 1903 with *The Mikado*, and then became a cinema with organ, a bingo hall and a night club.

Southgate, *c.* 1903. The palatial Borough Market on the right was designed by the Halifax architects Leeming and Leeming, who also designed Leeds City Market. Outward-facing shops, turrets and dormers and exterior ornamentation conceal the cast iron and glass interior. Opened in 1896 by the then Duke and Duchess of York (later George V and Queen Mary), the market and arcade fill the block between Southgate, Albion Street, Market Street and Russell Street.

Southgate, *c.* 1904. Much of the street was pedestrianised in 1973. It continues as Corn Market and Princess Street, giving a view of the Town Hall partly obscured by the White Swan Hotel. Southgate was widened, and the older buildings remain on the left, the west side.

Southgate, *c.* 1915. The street was widened between 1880–1910 and the new Arcade Royale built at King Edward Street corner.

King Edward Street. Situated between the Borough Market and Commercial Street, it is doubtless named after Edward VII, as parallel to it is Alexandra Street.

Above: Crown Street. A policeman is on duty in this busy shopping area, but where is the street traffic? Beacon Hill is in the distance.

Opposite above: Crown Street, *c.* 1904. It runs between Old Market and Cow Green, crossing the five-point junction with Silver, Commercial and Waterhouse Streets. This was the heart of old Halifax, on the route from Clark Bridge. Is the policeman on traffic duty?

Right: Crown Street, *c.* 1907. A view farther down is still without traffic, but has signs of horses and trams! Crown Street led down to Old Market and anciently to Gaol Lane, and also to Woolshops.

Below: Top of Woolshops. This old Stoddart's print presents a view from Market Street at Woolshops towards Old Market and Northgate. 'Woolshops' is thought to be a unique street-name.

Top of Woolshops, *c.* 1909. On the right, dated 1670, is the only remaining timber-framed house in town. It was restored during the 1983 Woolshops centre redevelopment, and its timbers exposed. In the past, horse traffic endured a steep pull from the station and canal terminus at Bank Bottom to Market Street.

Princess Street, *c.* 1905. This was part of the town centre improvement scheme of the 1880s and 1890s. This popular view is taken from the junction with Crown Street left and Old Market right, with the White Swan Hotel on the left far corner and Lipton's shop on the right.

Princess Street viewed from Corn Market, *c.* 1913. The Crown Street corner has Salmon and Gluckstein's shop on the left, while the Old Market corner has Lipton's. How many royal street names are there in the upper town centre?

Northgate. Gaol Lane reaches Northgate at Walkers shop and the cart on the right. Hepworth's clothiers are on the left and Walkers drapers on the right. My aunt Louisa used to get coats of excellent worsted that lasted for years from a Northgate corner shop, probably Hepworth's.

North Bridge and the Grand Theatre. The six-arched stone bridge of 1770 over the Hebble was replaced in 1871 by the two-arched iron bridge. At the Northgate end is a drinking fountain, a memorial to James Oates, one of the builders of the stone bridge. Opposite is the Grand Theatre and Opera House opened in 1889 with a canopy to shelter twice-nightly queues. It was demolished in 1954.

North Bridge, 2003. Now refurbished and brightly painted, it is in quieter use as it has been bypassed by a flyover.

four

Railways

North Bridge station goods yard. LMS ex-Lancashire and Yorkshire Railway's 0-6-0 class 3F number 12237 was an engine designed by Aspinall in 1889. 290 of these engines were still running in 1944. The three-wheeled vehicle on the left is a Mechanical Horse, introduced in the 1930s to replace horses for moving loads in goods yards. It had a small turning circle, like a real horse in shafts. (From the collection of Andy Johnson)

Halifax station. Beacon Hill looms up behind Baldwin's chimney while Mackintosh's appears above the hut on the right. This great hill consists of carboniferous coal measures capped by Elland Flags and extensively quarried around Hipperholme.

Halifax station. This third station and its approach road date from 1885. The older building of 1855
below the bridge is obscured by a canopy. The Great Northern lines veer off left to the Beacon Hill
tunnel entrance near Baldwins' mills. The Lancashire and Yorkshire continues towards North Bridge
and Ovenden. The Great Northern also had lines and stations at North Bridge, Holmfield, Pellon and
St Paul's.

Halifax's original station. Designed by Butterworth of Manchester, it was built in 1855 to replace
a temporary wooden station, and served both companies. Recent surface cleaning has restored it
to a golden glow. (Photo by Vera Chapman, 2002)

Pellon high level line: Pellon station, *c.* 1953. The bridge beyond the wagon is on Pellon Lane. Trains travelled under this to the island platform, behind the goods yard unloading crane. Young's timber yard siding was to the right. The water tower was still in use and Ken was one of the yard's staff. Three goods trains per day came on weekdays and two on Saturdays from Bradford. Around 1957 the locomotives were provided by Sowerby Bridge MPD. (Courtesy of Michael Schofield)

St Paul's terminus on a Sunday in the mid-1950s. A works train has come to remove a disused water tower. The engine, a J39 0-6-0, emits steam. A railway breakdown crane is engaged in dismantling the tower. The bridge mid-right carries Hopwood Lane, and Riley's Toffee Works and chimney are on the far side. The firm was taken over by Nuttall's Mintoes in the 1960s. The St Paul's line opened in 1890 and closed to passengers in 1917. (Courtesy of Michael Schofield)

The Wheatley Viaduct. The ten-arched viaduct and embankment carried the Pellon high level railway, a three-mile branch line of the Great Northern Railway across the Wheatley Valley from Holmfield to Pellon and St Paul's stations. The arches are reflected in the water below. (From the collection of Andy Johnson)

The Wheatley Viaduct, c. 1924. A minor road leads to a mill beyond. The main road curves off from the Wheatley Valley round the foot of Page Hill towards where the railway enters the Queensbury tunnel under the hill.

The 10614 Railmotor at Stainland, *c.* 1930. The Stainland branch line built in 1887 climbed up from the Calder Valley via Greetland. The over three miles journey took thirteen minutes each way between Halifax and Stainland in 1887 and cost 6d First Class and 3d Third Class. The all-in-one Railmotor, an 0-4-0 tank engine combined with a passenger coach, was designed by Hughes in 1906 for the Lancashire and Yorkshire Railway (later the LMS). At least 18 were built. Two were still operational in 1944. (From the collection of Andy Johnson)

The pier at Morecambe. Excursion trips from Halifax to Blackpool and Morecambe were run from Holmfield, Pellon and St Paul's stations on the Pellon high level branch railway.

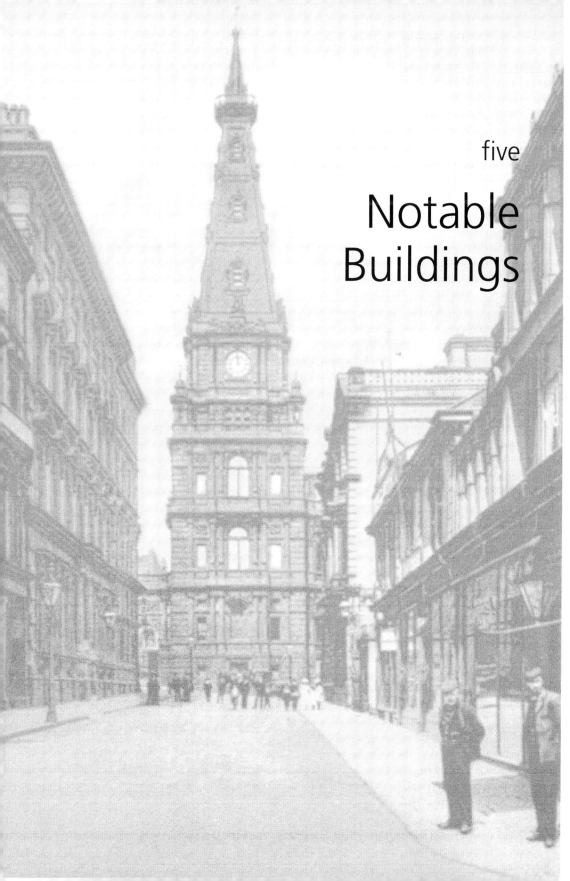

five

Notable
Buildings

Above: The parish church interior. The long chancel is underlain by a crypt. The font cover, of fifteenth century date, whose filigree tracery rises in tiers to a soaring spire, is especially fine. Seventeenth-century oak box pews were retained at the restoration but lowered. Galleries were removed. There are memorials to old local worthies, such as the Savile, Rokeby and Waterhouse families.

Opposite above: Halifax parish church, *c.* 1902. The Norman church of St John the Baptist was rebuilt in the Perpendicular style in the prosperous fifteenth century and a larger tower built. The church was restored in 1878-1879 by Sir George Gilbert Scott. The north aisle near the porch still shows Norman features of the early twelfth century but mainly dates from 1290. Saxon stones have been identified. St John's stands on the old way from Wakefield via Clark Bridge to Halifax, and historically served one of the largest parishes in England.

Right: Old Tristram. This life-sized figure stands near the door holding an alms box, a licensed beggar of the seventeenth century who worked in the church precincts. His plaque says: 'Pray Remember the Poor'. This figure was carved by John Aked.

Wakefield Cathedral. Halifax has been in the diocese of Wakefield since 1888. The former parish church of All Saints, Perpendicular in style on the exterior, was then enlarged. The crocketed spire with crocketed pinnacles is noted as the tallest in Yorkshire.

St Jude's church, *c.* 1904. This was built in 1889-1890 on the corner of Free School Lane and Savile Park Road, near the corner of Savile Park, formerly part of Skircoat Moor. It was designed in the Perpendicular style by W.S. Barber. The Baldwins of Clark Bridge Mills were benefactors. Novelist Phyllis Bentley attended. Her father was a churchwarden.

The Piece Hall, 1977. Built in 1770, this unique survival is a scheduled Ancient Monument. In prosperous times, hand-loom weavers sold their pieces of cloth from the 315 rooms. Water and steam-powered mills ousted the domestic industry. From 1868 it was a Corporation open-air fish and vegetable market. Restored in the 1970s, it has numerous uses as a market, textile museum, art gallery, crafts and for tourism. The spire is of the Square church.

Above: Detail from the South Gate, the Piece Hall, 1977. The open trading square had a central gateway on each side. These cast iron gates are from around 1903.

Right: Halifax Town Hall and Princess Street. The latter leads to Crossley Street, which passes in front of the Town Hall. These were part of John Crossley's plans for the area in 1851, together with his White Swan Hotel on the left, on the site of a coaching inn of that name. Next door is a former Halifax Permanent Benefit Building Society headquarters, built 1871–1873. Opposite the hotel is Princess Buildings.

The post office, *c.* 1905. Built in Commercial Street in local Yorkshire stone, it was designed by Henry Tanner, architect to the local Board of Works. Opened in 1887, it was enlarged in 1927 to accommodate a telephone exchange.

The post office, *c.* 1904. It faces the end of Rawson Street. This building was a popular subject for photographers. They often liked to include the pillars of the bank opposite.

The Halifax and Huddersfield Union Banking Company, *c.* 1909. Built in 1898 at an angle to Commercial Street opposite the post office, its imposing entrance portico has green Norwegian granite pillars. It now houses a branch of Lloyds–TSB bank.

The Victoria Hall, *c.* 1905. Built in 1900 in late Renaissance style for a private company at the south end of Commercial Street, it was designed by W. Clement Williams and opened for concerts in 1901. It could seat 2,660 people and house symphony orchestras. Bought by Halifax Corporation in 1960 it became the Civic Theatre and in 1993 the Victoria Theatre, opening again as it originally did with a Halle Orchestra concert. (See page 32).

Bankfield Museum and Library. Shortly before he died in 1887, Colonel Edward Akroyd sold his much enlarged villa and grounds to Halifax Corporation. The following year it was opened as a public museum, library and park.

Belle Vue Central Library and Museum. In French Renaissance style with a steep dormered roof, Belle Vue was built for Sir Francis Crossley in 1857 in Hopwood Lane. He died there in 1872. It was sold to Halifax Corporation for a nominal sum and in 1889 opened as a library and museum.

Heath grammar school, *c.* 1908. On the south side of Free School Lane the free grammar school of Queen Elizabeth was founded by Royal charter in 1585. In 1872 new stone Tudor-style buildings were completed. Several changes of status ensued, including a link with Crossley and Porter schools. The rose window of the original school building survived.

St Luke's Military Hospital. A new Poor Law hospital designed by W. Clement Williams opened at Salterhebble in 1901 with 900 beds. During the First World War it became a military hospital with temporary accommodation in the grounds. From the Second World War, St Luke's became Halifax General Hospital.

Halifax Royal Infirmary, *c.* 1918. Their Royal Highnesses, the Duke and Duchess of York opened this new infirmary in Free School Lane in 1896. It was designed by Worthington and Ellgood of Manchester, in Renaissance style. Six separate blocks joined by corridors were designed to reduce the spread of infection – a plan recommended by Florence Nightingale. Wards were named after their wealthy benefactors.

The orphanage, *c.* 1911. Now the Crossley Heath school, this massive pile on Skircoat Moor Road designed by John Hogg of Halifax, was built and jointly endowed as a school and orphanage by John, Joseph and Francis Crossley. Boys and girls from the age of seven were accepted from all parts of Britain. In 1887 Thomas Porter, a Manchester yarn merchant, donated a large sum to the endowment fund. By the end of the century, several hundred children were being clothed, fed and boarded until their mid-teens. After the First World War it became a secondary school and merged with Heath grammar school as the Crossley Heath school.

six

The West End

Savile Park. This former part of Skircoat Moor was acquired from the Savile family by Halifax Corporation in 1866. The drinking fountain was designed by John Hogg. The orphanage, far left, and more distant Wainhouse Tower appear. Limited eastward by the precipitous Beacon Hill, Halifax town spread westward up the gentler slopes where the prevailing westerlies ensured less smoke pollution and where old landowning families had left during industrialisation of the town. Large meets on the park included the Yorkshire Show.

Above: Well Head Lane, *c.* 1911: a quiet residential area off Savile Road half a mile out of town, developed from the late eighteenth century. Well Head House was built for the Waterhouses, woollen cloth merchants. Well Head Springs supplied water to the town until the age of moorland reservoirs. Water could be drunk there or collected to take away.

Opposite middle: A Christmas bookmark, 1929. This was sent to Liberal supporters. Sir George had unveiled the town's Cenotaph in Belle Vue grounds in 1922.

Opposite below: West View Park, *c.* 1908. Formerly known as Highroad Well Moor it was opened as a park in 1896 on high ground east of Cote Hill beside the Warley Road. It was laid out at the joint expense of two industrialists, Alderman Enoch Robinson and H.C. McCrea, and presented to the town. The balustrade used to stand beside Halifax Town Hall.

Above: The lower promenade and rocks, Halifax.

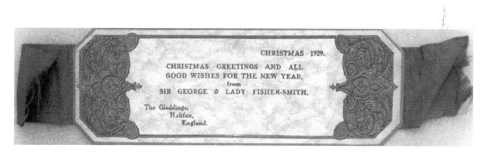

CHRISTMAS 1929.

CHRISTMAS GREETINGS AND ALL
GOOD WISHES FOR THE NEW YEAR,
from
SIR GEORGE & LADY FISHER-SMITH.

The Gleddings,
Halifax,
England.

Left: The Halifax Soldiers' Memorial, West View Park, *c.* 1906. It commemorates the South African Boer War, 1899-1902, and was unveiled in 1904 by Major Sir Leslie Rundle, KCB. There are views to as far west as Stoodley Pike.

Below: Cote Hill, *c.* 1928. This village lay just west of West View Park on the King Cross Lane-Burnley Road tramway to Sowerby Bridge. The little Early-English church of St John the Evangelist was built in 1878 for 342 sittings. I remember a childhood visit to a relative here one Christmas. She went into the back garden and killed a chicken for us to take back!

Above: Warley, or Warley Town. This village west of Cote Hill stands high above Sowerby Bridge. The Congregational church built in 1820 is now divided into dwellings. The fountain is inscribed: 'This drinking fountain was erected on the site of the old village maypole by A.S.M. McCrea of Warley House, AD 1900'. Just around the corner is the Maypole inn. Wilfred Pickles of radio's popular *Have a Go* programme once lived here. His wife Mable's recipes also became popular.

Right: The Wainhouse Tower, *c.* 1914. This ornamental tower which is 253ft high was built in 1871–1875 as a brick chimney for Edward Wainhouse's West Lane Dyeworks at the foot of The Rocks. An outer octagonal casing of stone from a quarry at the foot enclosed a spiral staircase of 403 steps which led past two viewing platforms up to four pedimented balconies. An entry for the dyeworks' flue is at the base of the tower. Isaac Booth was the architect, but after a dispute Wainwright sold the dyeworks to Richard Swarbrick Dugdale, the assistant architect, who redesigned the chimney top as a Renaissance-style observatory. The tower appears blackened no doubt by smoke from the mills in the valley below, but gritstone does tend to blacken on exposure.

The Rocks and Albert Promenade, *c.* 1914. This new road constructed on the former Skircoat Moor was opened in 1861, funded by local industrialists at the instigation of H.C. McCrea. Its spectacular views reach over the mills of Sowerby Bridge to Copley Woods and Norland opposite, and west to Sowerby village, the Calder Valley and the high Pennines around Blackstone Edge.

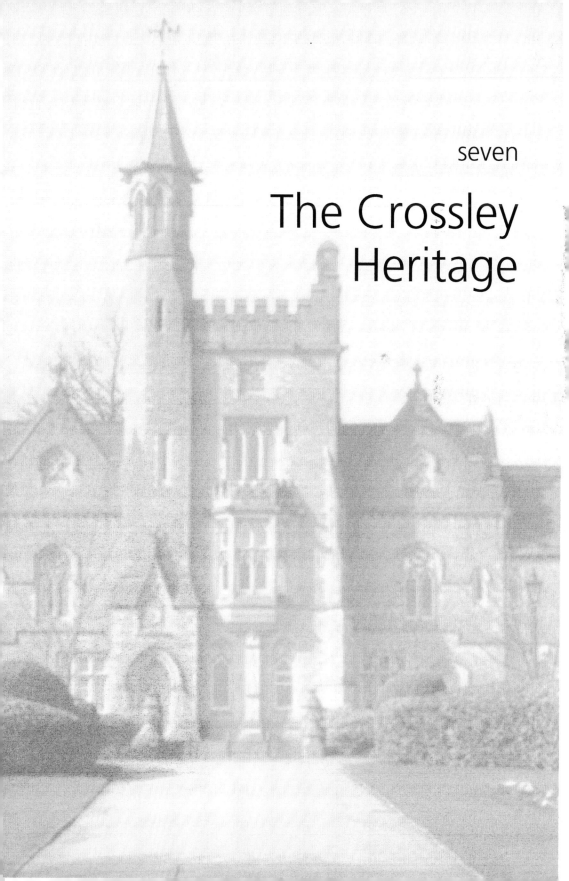

seven

The Crossley Heritage

Belle Vue and garden. John Crossley and Sons became the world's largest carpet manufacturers, and enormously wealthy. Their Dean Clough Mills covered about thirty acres and employed nearly 6,000 people. John's home was Manor Heath in the West End. He had three sons; John, Joseph and Francis. Belle Vue was the home of Sir Francis. First built in 1848 it was given its French classical style in 1856, with steep roofs and a central pavilion roof. The house and grounds were sold to Halifax Corporation in 1889, and the town's library and museum used it until 1983. The First World War Cenotaph was sited there. From the 1990s a business group is based there and it has been renamed Crossley House.

Belle Vue. This view shows the main entrance portico which has a coffered roof with a balcony over. The architect was George Henry Stokes. The mansion faces Hopwood Lane and the People's Park, which Sir Francis created as a gift to the town.

Belle Vue. The gardens, terrace, tower and wall (presumably a walled garden or conservatory) hide a nearby church.

Sir Francis Crossley's almshouses, *c.* 1910. In 1855 Francis built and endowed twenty-two almshouses facing Margaret Street and backing on to the grounds of Belle Vue, which is just visible on the left. Using a Gothic style with towers at each end, the architect was Roger Ives. Occupants had to be poor and of good character, and adhere to church doctrine. They received a weekly endowment allowance.

Sir Francis Crossley's almshouses, 2002. They stretch between Hopwood Lane and Lister Lane, and face Margaret Street. Their recent restoration reveals the golden glow of the sandstone. To the right, or east, is the West Hill Park estate, streets of workers' terraced homes built by John Crossley junior, from 1864. (Photo Vera Chapman)

Joseph Crossley's almshouses, 2002. These forty-eight almshouses were built in 1863-1870 in Tudor style in Arden Road, between King Cross Road and Savile Park Road as an east-facing open square at the opposite end of Peoples' Park from Francis's almshouses. The architect was Roger Ives. This view from the entrance gates shows only a part of the main range. (Vera Chapman)

Park Congregational church, Hopwood Lane. The Scout officials and the cub pack pose for a photograph. Scouts included here are, on the left Colin Park and on the right Michael Schofield. (Courtesy of Michael Schofield)

Park Congregational church, Hopwood Lane, *c.* 1947. On the back row the Scout with the Union Jack is Frank Park who later emigrated to Australia, and on the second row from the front, fourth from the right, is Michael Schofield, while on the front row, fourth from the left is Colin Park who later emigrated to Canada. (Courtesy of Michael Schofield)

Above: Square Congregational churches, 2003. The first Square church was built of brick in 1772, and became a Sunday school when the Gothic church of 1857 was built alongside, right, seating 1200. The tower and slender 235 feet spire were financed by Sir Francis Crossley, and John Crossley junior was a deacon and chairman of the building committee. The new church closed in 1970, was greatly fire-damaged in 1972 and mostly demolished in 1977. The landmark spire survives (see page 50).

Left: Sir Savile and Lady Crossley, *c.* 1906. This portrait photograph is reproduced on a postcard. The message reads: 'Liberals have got in here. It as [*sic*] caused a lot of excitement.'

Opposite below: The orphanage, *c.* 1903. John junior, Joseph and Francis Crossley jointly made a substantial contribution to the building in 1864 and the endowment of this massive orphanage and school on the corner of Savile Park. Thomas Porter in 1887 also made a large donation. It became known as the Crossley and Porter school.

Above: Town Hall and White Swan Hotel. John Crossley junior's plans for the Town Hall were carried against opposition, especially from Akroyd supporters. The White Swan Hotel was built for him in 1858, to accommodate visiting businessmen. Crossley House behind and below the Town Hall was the Crossley firm's town centre office and showroom. The street across the front of the pyramidal spire is Crossley Street.

Above: Crossley and Porter schools, *c.* 1911. This clear view shows the long frontage.

Left: Sir Francis (Frank) Crossley. This statue of Carrara marble by Joseph Durham, the centrepiece of the pavilion on the terrace of the People's Park, was subscribed for in 1860 by the people of Halifax. The inscription reads: 'This statue of Frank Crossley Esquire, MP for the West Riding of York, donor of the Peoples' Park was erected August 14, 1866 by the inhabitants of Halifax his native town as a tribute of gratitude and respect to one whose public benefactions and private virtues Deserve to be Remembered'.

eight

The People's Park

The terrace, pavilion and statuary, *c.* 1930. Belle Vue, Sir Francis' home, is in the background. He preferred to be called Frank. The terrace and pavilion were designed by George Henry Stokes, the son-in-law and assistant to Sir Joseph Paxton, designer of the Crystal Palace, who laid out the park for Sir Francis from five flat fields between Hopwood Lane and King Cross Street. It opened in 1857.

The People's Park in bloom, *c.* 1904.

Above: The bridge, lake and Sir Francis's almshouses tower, *c.* 1907.

Opposite below: The Italian-style pavilion has two wings with fountains surmounted by inscriptions: 'Let no man seek his own but every man another's wealth' and 'The rich and poor meet together. The Lord is the Maker of them all'. In the centre is 'Blessed be the Lord who daily loadeth us with Benefits.'

People at leisure, *c.* 1910. Note the pram and bassinette near the sundial 'donated to the People's Park in the year 1873 by Alderman Matthew Smith, erected 1879'. It is also inscribed: 'Time by moments steals away, first the hour, then the day'.

The new bandstand erected in 1897, seen here around 1904. Substantial terraced houses face the park.

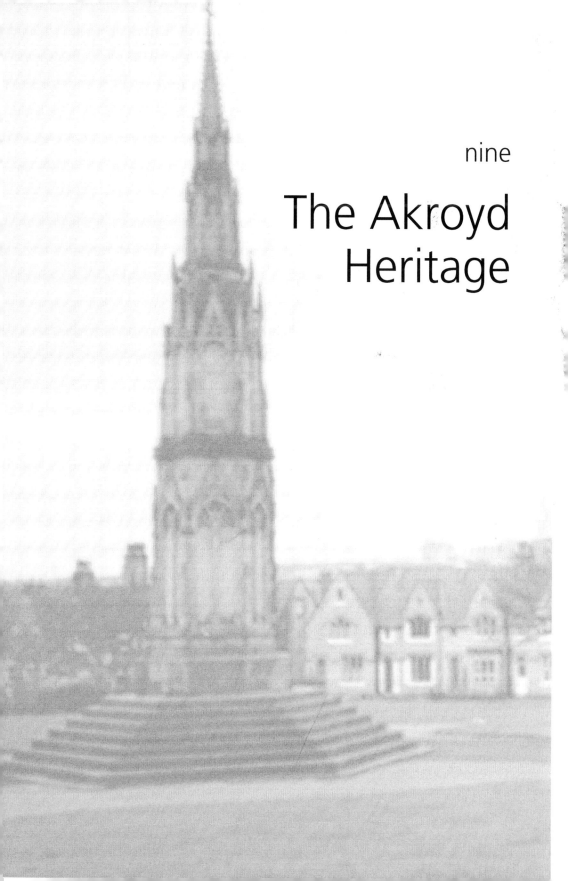

nine

The Akroyd Heritage

The ornamental fountain at Akroyd Park. It has since been filled in. The museum itself housed the bust of a Veiled Lady, her facial features showing through a veil draped over her face and shoulders, all carved in white marble.

Akroyd Park, c. 1916. A terrace with seating next to a drinking fountain allowed a view of All Souls down the steep hillside. The area up Haley Hill was old Boothtown, and became Akroydon.

Above left: Colonel Edward Akroyd (1810-1887), mill owner and philanthropist. This statue marked his retirement as MP, and formerly stood on North Bridge. It now looks towards his mills in the Hebble Brook Valley. He holds a plan of his model village, Akroydon. The panels illustrate events in his life.

Above right: All Souls church. Built and endowed by Colonel Akroyd in 1856-1889, it was designed by Sir George Gilbert Scott who regarded it as 'on the whole my best church' (Pevsner). Built one year later than Crossley's Square church, Akroyd's spire at 236ft is one foot taller! Built of Millstone grit but unfortunately encased in magnesian limestone which has crumbled dangerously, All Souls church is now closed.

Left: Woodside Crescent, 1992. 'Woodside' was a villa across the Haley Hill Road from Bankfield, built in 1825 for Edward's father Jonathan. Other Akroyds lived there until 1897 when it was sold and the grounds built over in parallel terraces with small back and front gardens. Woodside Baths, built in 1893, have been demolished.

Bankfield, *c.* 1910. On his marriage in 1838, Colonel Edward Akroyd, a worsted manufacturer, bought a small Georgian house near his Haley Hill Mills. This he enlarged in stages into a magnificent Italian villa with a porte cochère, grand marble staircase and frescoes. Eventually he sold it to Halifax Corporation, which from around 1887 developed it as Bankfield Museum, Art Gallery and Branch Library and its grounds into a public park.

St Stephen's Street, Copley, 2002. Edward Akroyd had built his first model village at Copley in 1849-1853 for his woollen mill of 1847, which has since been demolished. The houses are in long rows of back-to-backs with front gardens. He also built a school, library and church.

Akroydon, 1992. From 1861 Edward built further houses at Boothtown, planned for two sets of terraces facing a square green, with a central Queen Victoria Cross modelled on the famous Queen Eleanor Cross. Allotments were provided.

The initials of early homeowners, 2002. The village was planned by Sir George Gilbert Scott and built in conjunction with the Halifax Permanent Building Society.

Left: The Akroydon houses vary in size and design, and are more ornate than those near All Souls, some of which appear to have been back-to-backs.

Below: Shroggs Park. Colonel Akroyd recognised that Lee Mount, a wooded promontory across the Hebble Valley, could be an amenity for his Akroydon families. In 1881 it was given to Halifax Corporation by Captain Savile and laid out as a park at the Colonel's expense.

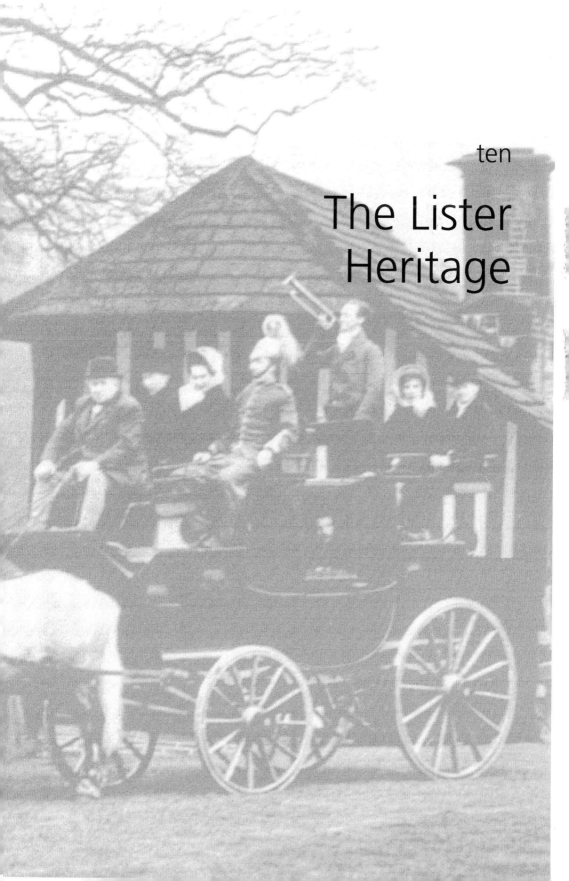

ten

The Lister
Heritage

Shibden Hall, *c.* 1901. This timber-framed hall, an Ancient Monument, was built in around 1420 by William Oates. It was owned by the Lister family from 1619 for around 300 years until being bought by A.S. McCrea, who gifted the grounds in 1923 as a public park. When John Lister the antiquarian died in 1933 the house passed to Halifax Corporation and became a museum.

Shibden Hall, *c.* 1921. In the seventeenth century, parts of the front were encased in stone. In the early nineteenth century Anne Lister added a tower and wing. The long low window is Elizabethan and the interiors are oak-panelled. It has been described as 'the oldest and most gracious of the great houses now in the town's possession'.

Reception hall or 'house body'. Entered from the porch between the two wings, it has a huge fireplace and black and white walls above a panelled dado. The Elizabethan window has nine mullions. Seventeenth and eighteenth-century furniture once belonging to the Lister family is used. (The interior and park photographs are courtesy of Frank Atkinson)

The Dining Room. The rooms are furnished as they may have been in the early years of the Listers.

The Savile Room.

The four-poster bed with tester.

Shibden Hall Park, *c.* 1934. The fifteenth-century timber-framed cottage by the lake was rescued from Cripplegate near Halifax parish church by John Lister, and re-erected here for safe keeping. Following neglect, it was demolished in 1971.

The Lister post-chaise in Shibden Park. The park was formally opened in 1926 by the Prince of Wales who planted a young oak tree.

Above: A stage coach, beside the Cripplegate timber-framed cottage.

Left: Frank Atkinson. After service at Wakefield Museum Frank became the director (1951–1958) of Halifax museums, Bankfield, Shibden and Belle Vue, moving on to be director of the Bowes Museum at Barnard Castle until 1970. He then became the founding director of Beamish North of England Open Air Museum, which he masterminded and virtually created.

Opposite below: An aisled barn. Frank found and rescued a decaying stone barn built in 1670, with a cruck-framed, heather-thatched roof. He re-erected it at Shibden, though unfortunately it later burnt down when the dry thatch caught fire.

Above: The wheelwright's shop, Shibden Hall Folk Museum. Frank was acutely aware of rapid change. He also realised that qualities unique to the Halifax district were disappearing. Thus he set about to explore, record and rescue, developing, alongside Shibden Hall, the Folk Museum of West Yorkshire.

Coal-mining horse gin. This apparatus was once common for small-scale mining of shallow coal seams in the Shibden Valley and moorlands. A horse walked round winding the rope on to the drum to raise a load of coals from the mine. On demolition, the contraption left puzzling circular marks on the land. Frank rescued this example from Rothwell.

Judd wall, 1952. The recording of social history was a prime interest. Frank soon appointed his first museum assistant, art-trained Joan Peirson, who later became his wife. Here they are above Boothtown, recording a 'judd wall'; a local means of supporting a track or road on the steep hillsides of Halifax and Calderdale.

Left: Old houses at Boothtown. (Photograph by Frank Atkinson, courtesy of the Beamish Museum Archive Record)

Below: Frank Helliwell and his sister. Seen here haymaking at Sands Farm, a small hillside holding above Boulder Clough near Luddenden Foot. They tied each bundle with rope and carried it on their heads to the 'hay-mow' or hay barn at the steading. He was known locally as 'Frank o' Sands'.

Above: Verney Horsfall, clogger, Hebden Bridge, 1957. He was the last clogger in the Calder Valley. Frank Atkinson made a 16mm colour film of the many skills involved in making a clog hand-crafted to fit each individual foot. Verney enabled a completely equipped clogger's shop to be assembled at Shibden Hall Folk Museum.

Left: Barkisland Hall. This more than usually-ornate façade graces a 'Halifax House', a type typical of the numerous seventeenth-century homes on the hillsides around the town and extensive parish of Halifax, of which Frank had noted 200 examples. Barkisland was completed in 1638 for John and Sarah Gledhill. (Photo by H.P. Kendall, courtesy of Beamish Museum, via Frank Atkinson)

eleven

Shibden Dale

Stump Cross, *c.* 1910. At the bridge over Shibden Brook the A649 road on an embankment turns sharp right past the Museum Hotel towards Hipperholme. Until the 1820s, the old road went down to the brook then up and over the hill end. The small building on the right looks like a toll booth.

Sunny Vale, Hipperholme, *c.* 1930. Nicknamed Sunny Bunces, this pleasure ground was opened in 1883 by Joseph Bunce and run by his family until 1945, closing soon after. There was dancing, carnivals and bands, and a park with two large lakes for boating, steamer trips and winter skating. Eric Harrison, a Heath Grammar School prodigy pianist, is seen here with me in the boat. He eventually became a senior lecturer in piano at Melbourne University.

Left: Sunny Vale, *c.* 1930. Swings and cornets were enjoyed on this day. My grandma Taylor is on the left. The Taylor and Harrison grandparents were friends, both families living on the Woodside estate at Boothtown.

This scene shows hillside disturbance, and a sheerlegs or derrick for hoisting quarried stone appears on the hilltop above a spoil tip. An eighteenth-century traveller, Bishop Richard Pococke, on travelling from Keighley to Halifax, recorded that the hills rise above Halifax 'not unlike the Mount of Olives over Jerusalem, and all the hills are full of coals'.

bankment, Ogden, Halifax.

Ogden, *c.* 1913. Across from the head of Shibden Dale is Ogden Reservoir which dams the head of the parallel Hebble Brook. In 1901, Halifax Golf Club set up a nine-hole course south of the reservoir and screened from it by plantations on Spice Cake Hills. Rich fruit cake in West Yorkshire is called spice cake, and should be eaten with cheese! The club house was built in 1902 and soon the course was extended to eighteen holes.

Opposite above: Shibden Dale, north of Stump Cross. This apparently rural scene included Shibden Mill inn 1643 and Dam Head – a timber-framed aisled hall and a seventeenth-century house. The mill has been demolished. On the hillside is disturbed ground: Anne Lister developed coal mining on her estate, and fireclay bands were also mined extensively, while flagstones were quarried at Hipperholme and Beacon Hill.

Opposite below: Illingworth. This substantial settlement on high ground between the upper Hebble and Shibden Brooks near Ovenden is only three miles from Halifax town centre. St Mary's church was simple until the Venetian East window was added in 1888. The nearby stocks are dated 1697. The lock-up dated 1823 pleaded: 'Let him that stole steal no more but rather let him labour working with his hands the thing which is good, that he may give to him that needeth'. The tram is mounting Wrigley Hill on the Keighley-Halifax road (A629).

Ringby, in the upper Shibden Valley. The A647 from Haley Hill and Boothtown passes Ringby Farm and Ringby Lane. This view looks towards Swalesmoor inn across a typical rural industrial settlement. Behind the photographer is Holmfield where fireclay for lining furnaces was processed from numerous small mines.

Limed House, Shibden, alternatively known as Lime House.

twelve

Moorlands

Ogden Reservoir, *c.* 1913. It was built in 1854–1858, designed by J.F.Bateman of Brighouse and is now owned by Yorkshire Water. In the ring of valley heads between Burnley, Keighley, Huddersfield and Rochdale, about seventy reservoirs were built, while Halifax took the valley heads between it and Colne. Impervious rocks, heavy rainfalls released slowly by the peat yielded soft lime-free water, an asset for textile industries. Ogden became and still is a popular recreation area. As a youngster I used to come with my aunt and picked pounds of bilberries, returning with purple-stained hands.

Weir Falls, Ogden Kirk, *c.* 1907. The Ogden area is popular for recreational walking and family outings. The woodlands of Scots Pine with Larch and Birch allow nature interests and bird watching. Reservoir siting depends on the catchment area, rainfall and the geology of the valley floor and dam site. The best sites have the greatest storage capacity for the least constructional work and cost!

Bottoms Mill, Ogden. This spinning mill was built in the early 1800s. A small dam impounded a reserve of water which was then directed by a channel to the water wheel, whose position can just be seen. Ogden's wind farm on Ovenden Moor was built in 1993 with twenty-three wind towers providing power for over 7,000 homes.

Peat Pits inn, Ogden. I remember seeing the Peat Pits inn beside the main road and note that it is still named on the A629 in the Ordnance Survey Street Atlas.

Walker's 'Costumes of Yorkshire', 1814. Peat was dug by pressing a special peat spade with right-angled blades into a vertical peat bank and piling the peat in loose 'ruckles' to dry. These were then carted in barrows with no back or sides to dry in tidy rows. (Courtesy of Darlington Borough Library)

Above: The Moor Guide. Walker, 1814. The moors could be dangerous for wet and wild weather, mists, snow and ice, bogs, invisible tracks and robbers, so moor guides used to be hired. This house and heather-thatched barn were on Stainmore. My father used to refer to 'those moors' in an ominous voice when we travelled between Manchester and Halifax. Two of my family funerals across to Mount Tabor chapel on Highroad Well Moor had to be postponed because of Pennine snow.

Right: Slotted gatepost. Lower moorland commons were slowly enclosed in the sixteenth to eighteenth centuries, and later by Acts of Parliament. New fields had to be gated. Early gates were just bars slotted into post-holes at one side and L-shaped or curved slots on the opposite post. (Photo Vera Chapman)

Below right: Holed gatepost. (Photo Vera Chapman)

Opposite below: Cutting the peat. A few hill farmers with rights of common still dig peat, especially in difficult times. The practice long survived in the North York Moors using traditional methods. (Photo Vera Chapman)

The Ladstone Rock, Norland Moor, *c.* 1927. Norland, across the Calder from Halifax, bears this layered and weathered residual rock. Strange places attract legends – here the Druids.

The Moors and White Wells, Ilkley, *c.* 1912. Need one be reminded of the song *On Ilkley Moor Baht 'At*?

Haworth, *c.* 1913. Moorland scenes in West Yorkshire inevitably invoke the image of the Brontës and the haunting presence of *Wuthering Heights*. The 'bleak heather moors whose wildness entered into the very souls of the Brontë sisters' characterise West Yorkshire, as do the abrupt precipitous valleys of the Halifax district which an old-time wanderer, Taylor, 'the Water Poet' described as the 'lande of Breake-necke'.

The inn and church gates, Haworth. The steep street and the distant views of moorland beyond are characteristic of Haworth. In Halifax some mill women were still wearing shawls in the 1930s.

Main Street, Haworth. The stepped pavements and descending rooflines reflect the steepness. The street would not be so quiet now, in honey-pot tourism times.

thirteen

Along the
Calder Valley

Ravensthorpe, near Heckmondwike. Looking down on Ravensthorpe, the mills crowding along the Calder Valley bottom can be seen, a scene typical of the district with enclosed pastures on the lower slopes and rough moorland aloft. Ravensthorpe is on the north side of the river Calder and the Calder and Hebble Navigation. The station and Lady Wood are on the south side.

THE PARK, RAVENSTHORPE.

Holroyd Park, Ravensthorpe. An attractive local park where here, one man at least is ready for tennis!

THE PARK, RAVENSTHORPE.

Holroyd Park, Ravensthorpe. A seat for two is occupied. A terrace of good brick houses faces the park.

The Church of the Resurrection at Battyford, Mirfield. The Holy Cross chapel and Gore Memorial chantry. This is the Mother House of the Anglican College of the Order of the Resurrection, founded in 1892. The large church of red sandstone in Norman style was begun in 1911 by Sir Walter Tapper. The nave and aisles were built in 1937, designed by Michael Tapper. There is much tunnel vaulting, plain pillars and arches, and a crypt church below the nave. The college buildings date from 1905.

The Calvary Garden, Church of the Resurrection at Battyford, Mirfield. The college buildings of 1905 were designed by the Revd C.J. Ritson. There are several later additions. The original manufacturer's house on the site was retained.

Heckmondwike Market Place. Market Street, High Street and Westgate meet here. A horse and light cart stand on the left by the elaborate railed clock tower and lamp. The Red Lion public house is on the left, and Lumbard's Coffee Palace is next door to Joe Allott, undertaker.

Fieldhead of *Shirley*, *c.* 1923. Charlotte Brontë's novel *Shirley* is set in the Heckmondwike and Liversedge area. Shirley Keeldar's 'dark old manor house, the gallery and low-ceiled chambers that open into it, the dim entrance hall with its one window' are thought to be based on this house, and that the Georgian church at Liversedge built for the dedicated church builder the Revd H. Roberson in 1812–1816 was the model for the Revd H. Helstone in the novel.

Throstle Nest, Rastrick, *c.* 1906. My cousin, Capt. Clarence Park, lived for a while in Rastrick. There is an eleventh-century cross base in the churchyard.

Southgate, Elland, *c.* 1907. On the south bank of the Calder opposite Halifax, Elland was still defined as a woollen manufacturing town after the Second World War. A Charter of Edward II had been granted to John de Elland for a free market on Tuesdays, and two fairs. The market had been 'discontinued for generations' by the early nineteenth century, but a small market place and cross remained.

The Cross, Elland, *c.* 1915. Here is the main shopping area. There are substantial nineteenth-century buildings, including the Town Hall of 1888 designed by C.F.L. Horsfall of Halifax, with shops on the ground floor and an assembly hall and balcony above seating over 1,000. In the vicinity, several seventeenth-century halls testify to an earlier prosperity.

The Bridge, Elland, *c.* 1912. The main industries were woollen, worsted and cotton spinning, fireclay goods and sanitary pipes, wire-making and carding engines. There were also an iron and dyeworks and several maltings. The surrounding area produced excellent fireclay and stone, including Elland flags from the lower coal measures quarried for flagstones and crushing for Non-Slip artificial stone.

Elland from Nab End, *c.* 1905. The Calder and Hebble Navigation is on the left and the River Calder is on the right, with mills strung out along the valley bottom. The Calder and Hebble Navigation connected to the east coast and the Rochdale Canal to the west. The Halifax branch canal from Salterhebble to Clark Bridge via the lower Hebble Valley needed fourteen locks.

Above: Copley Woods. These were an amenity for Colonel Edward Akroyd's mill workers at his model village, tucked into a sharp curve of the Calder below Savile Park. Copley railway station is the next one to Sowerby bridge. In 1987 the Halifax Building Society opened its data centre at Wakefield Road, Copley.

Left: Norland, *c.* 1920. Norland Town and Norland Moor are in the angle between the Calder and the Ryburn Valleys near their confluence at Sowerby Bridge. The precipitous valleys were deepened during the Ice Age, at the end of which they were partially filled here by gravel. A long-distance footpath now runs along the top of the riverside woods and over Norland Moor.

Above: Sowerby. The old village typically perches high above the Calderdale slopes. The stately church of St Peter, seen here from Towngate, was built in 1763–1766 and its tower in 1781. There was a statue to Archbishop Tillotson, born at Haugh End. A medieval castle for hunting and hawking is recalled at Castle Hill Farm dated 1662. The Travellers' Rest on the right, with an address as Steep Lane, seems to have a stage coach sign.

Right: The Old Bar House, Sowerby, *c.* 1918. The Halifax and Rochdale Turnpike Road of 1734 via Blackstone Edge was followed by the Calder and Hebble Canal from Halifax to Sowerby Bridge in 1765, where in 1802 the Rochdale Canal linked with it. Then came the Lancashire and Yorkshire Railway, trams in 1902 and Ripponden and District buses to Oldham and Manchester in the 1920s and 1930s. Calderdale was and is an important through route.

Sowerby Bridge station. These buildings opened in 1876. A pack-horse bridge survives near the probably seventeenth-century main river bridge. Scribbling and worsted mills, corn mills, malt kilns, iron foundries and chemical works lined the riverside and canal-side wharves. The thirty-two mile Rochdale Canal from Manchester to Sowerby Bridge was nicknamed the 'Everest of Canals'. It lifted boatloads of coal, wood and salt 600ft through ninety-one locks! Our family bus journeys to Halifax began at the Rochdale Canal Yard in Manchester.

Triangle, *c.* 1917. This small settlement is on the west bank of the Ryburn River in an attractive side valley.

Luddenden Foot, *c.* 1916. The old village of Luddenden was superseded by industrial development at Luddenden Foot where the Luddenden Dene joins the Calder. The old village had two good seventeenth-century houses and a seventeenth-century inn incongruously named the Lord Nelson!

Hebden Bridge. At the confluence of the Hebden Water with the Calder it was well known in the early nineteenth century for its cotton mills near the canal, especially for fustian, a thick twilled short-napped cotton cloth and other hard-wearing cloths like corduroy and cavalry twill. This developed into a clothing industry for working men's clothes and riding breeches. It also became the terminus of the longest Halifax Corporation tram route.

Cragg Road, Mytholmroyd.

Mytholmroyd. Here – where Cragg Brook joins the Calder – was the birthplace in 1930 of Ted Hughes, son of a carpenter. He left here aged seven and went on to become a Cambridge graduate in 1954, soon to enter a famously volatile marriage with the American poetess Sylvia Plath. He was appointed Poet Laureate in 1984. He returned to the district, but died in 1998 and is buried in Devon.

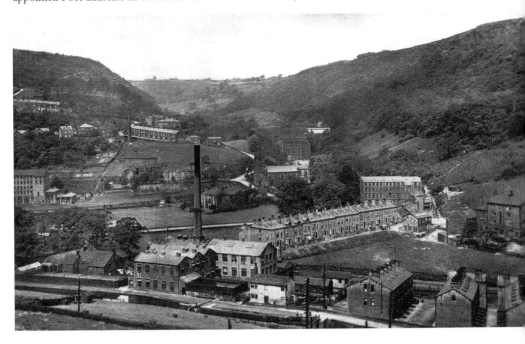

Mytholm and the Colden Valley. The upper Calder Valley included many small hamlets and scattered houses which evolved into industrial settlements. 1,000 acres of moors and commons were enclosed by an Act of Parliament in 1815. Mytholm chapel was built in 1835.

Two parish churches, *c.* 1931. The parish churches of Heptonstall and Hebden Bridge can be seen in one view. The former stands on the flat hilltop reached by a precipitously steep, narrow and twisting road, the latter on the flat valley floor of the upper Calder.

Above: Heptonstall, *c.* 1905. Two churches of the same parish stand side by side in one churchyard. The village is perched on a flat spur of land between the Colden Water and the Hebden Water valleys. It was originally a handloom weaving village. The old church of St Thomas was dismantled in 1854 and left as a ruin. The west tower was thirteenth century, the rest all Perpendicular. The new church of 1854 is also in the Perpendicular style, but the interior has been stripped of its Victorian pews and given a modern layout. Sylvia Plath, (1932-1963), wife of the Poet Laureate Ted Hughes, is buried in the graveyard. The grammar school of 1642 is now a museum. The Long Causeway leads over the moors to Burnley.

Left: Setts. These clean, gritty, little-worn sandstone setts in Heptonstall are a reminder of the streets of the Halifax district as they used to be, in towns and in villages.

The Lodge, Hardcastle Crags, *c.* 1912. Old quarries, former charcoal burning hearths and a packhorse track indicate a busy past in this present-day National Trust beauty spot. Gibson's Mill, built in 1800 for textiles, became a nineteenth-century dance hall and roller-skating rink with a pavilion tea room. Later abandoned, it is now restored for visitors. It used to be reached by tram or train to Hebden Bridge, then by horse-drawn vehicles.

Above: Stepping stones, Hardcastle Crags, *c.* 1907. Riverside walks and a nature trail lead up the wooded Hebden Dale to Hardcastle Crags. Bluebells and ramsons (*allium ursinum*) carpet the woods in season. Paths link with other footpaths and the Pennine Way. It is now the route of the Hebden Bridge to Haworth Walk over Ovenden Moor.

Left: Stoodley Pike. This obelisk was erected on a hilltop at 1,400ft to commemorate the defeat of Napoleon and the end of the Napoleonic and Crimean Wars. It is on the Pennine Way, and several rights of way lead up to it from Hebden Bridge and Mytholmroyd.

fourteen

Pellon and Woodside People

Above: An outing in 1929. This chapter is a small selection from my family albums to give a flavour of the period around the First World War. Ordinary families gradually recovered after the war and the great Depression, and fashions in dress altered. Standing on the right are my parents John and Florence Taylor of Woodside. He returned to his work at the *Halifax Courier* and married Florence, who had lost her fiancé in the war.

Left: Lucy Taylor of Woodside Crescent who died in 1946 aged eighty-three, after suffering a stroke playing competition bowls on a hot day in Akroyd Park. She had been a keen Liberal supporter and a charity worker with mothers and children.

Above left: James (Jim) Taylor, Lucy's husband who died in 1949 aged ninety. He moved to Halifax during the great cotton depression of the late nineteenth century. I saw him once at work in the entrance lodge of Akroyd's Haley Hill mill.

Above right: Harry, born 1887, and John, born 1885, sons of James and Lucy.

Right: John Taylor. He volunteered on 24 October 1914 and served as a Private in the West Yorkshire Regiment, becoming a member of the Army Cyclist' Corps, who carried messages across the battlefields of the Western Front. He got PUO (Pyrexia of Unknown Origin – probably 'trench fever') and convalesced in Tipperary.

John Taylor's cap badge of the Army Cyclists' Corps. He returned to the *Halifax Courier* after the war.

Above left: Florence Dewhirst of a Pellon family of three sisters. She remembered being allowed to stand up on desks or chairs, probably at Pellon Lane school, to watch the first tramcar go by! She later became a commercial clerk.

Above right: Albert Hargreaves, a Halifax policeman. He served with the 4th Grenadier Guards, but died from wounds in France. He and Florence were engaged, but decided to wait until the war was over.

Right: Harry Taylor and Phyllis, his wife. Harry trained as a cabinet maker. He volunteered for the West Yorkshire Regiment, became a sergeant and a Pioneer, keeping roads in repair to support front-line troops. He was killed in action on 1 November 1918 in the battle for Valenciennes, and received the DCM. He knew that his wife had died in the 1918 'flu pandemic and his only child of diphtheria.

Memorial plaque.

Above left: Louisa Dewhirst, Florence's elder sister. She worked in a nearby mill until she was sixty, leaving at 5.30 a.m. and returning for breakfast at 7.30 a.m. Her house in Hartley Street, Pellon, was a cosy back-to-back, with a piano and a cat called Omar that liked the sultanas out of scones, a corner gas ring and sink cupboard, and a 'peggy' rug by the iron range, a flush toilet in the cellar and an attic where I slept on visits.

Above right: Louisa Dewhirst in retirement. She died in 1952 aged seventy-six, and was buried in the family grave at Mount Tabor. En route, the hearse was covered with snow.

Right: Will Sutcliffe, a boyhood friend of John, at his 1920s wedding. They 'emigrated' to Manchester, where he managed a high-class furniture shop. The Taylor and Sutcliffe exiles kept in touch.

Acknowledgements

My sincere thanks go to those who have helped me in the preparation of this collection, either with information or with the loan of old photographs with permission to copy. I have taken advice as to dating and copyright.

The book is based mainly on my own collection of Edwardian postcards, for many of which I am grateful to the traders and collectors who had saved them for posterity. I have included photographs from my inherited family albums, as a basis for personal memories of the town, people, events and incidents in my younger-day connections with Halifax.

For photographs I am especially indebted to Dr Frank Atkinson CBE, former Director of Halifax Museums, who has allowed me to include a generous number of his own. I thank also Brian Notarianni of Coats Craft UK, Michael Schofield and Andy Johnson. They and Joan Atkinson, Betty Gaunt and Peter Schofield also gave me the benefit of their recollections.

My husband Ken and sons Tim and Andy have assisted in various supportive ways. Darlington Borough Library has, as always, been helpful in supplying background reading, among which I especially mention the valuable work of John Hargreaves and Stephen Gee.